THE GRAPES OF WRATH

John Steinbeck

SPARKNOTES is a registered trademark of SparkNotes LLC

This edition published by Spark Publishing

Spark Publishing
A Division of SparkNotes LLC
120 Fifth Avenue, 8th Floor
New York, NY 10011

Please submit all comments and questions or report errors to www.sparknotes.com/errors

Printed and bound in the United States

ISBN 1-58663-360-0

INTRODUCTION:
STOPPING TO BUY
SPARKNOTES ON A
SNOWY EVENING

Whose words these are you *think* you know.
Your paper's due tomorrow, though;
We're glad to see you stopping here
To get some help before you go.

Lost your course? You'll find it here.
Face tests and essays without fear.
Between the words, good grades at stake:
Get great results throughout the year.

Once school bells caused your heart to quake
As teachers circled each mistake.
Use SparkNotes and no longer weep,
Ace every single test you take.

Yes, books are lovely, dark, and deep,
But only what you grasp you keep,
With hours to go before you sleep,
With hours to go before you sleep.

Contents

CONTEXT

JOHN STEINBECK was born in Salinas, California, on February 27, 1902. He attended Stanford University without graduating, and though he lived briefly in New York, he remained a lifelong Californian. Steinbeck began writing novels in 1929, but he garnered little commercial or critical success until the publication of *Tortilla Flat* in 1935. Steinbeck frequently used his fiction to delve into the lives of society's most downtrodden citizens. A trio of novels in the late 1930s focused on the lives of migrant workers in California: *In Dubious Battle,* published in 1936, was followed by *Of Mice and Men* in 1937, and, in 1939, Steinbeck's masterpiece, *The Grapes of Wrath.*

During the early 1930s, a severe drought led to massive agricultural failure in parts of the southern Great Plains, particularly throughout western Oklahoma and the Texas panhandle. These areas had been heavily overcultivated by wheat farmers in the years following World War I and were covered with millions of acres of loose, exposed topsoil. In the absence of rain, crops withered and died; the topsoil, no longer anchored by growing roots, was picked up by the winds and carried in billowing clouds across the region. Huge dust storms blew across the area, at times blocking out the sun and even suffocating those unlucky enough to be caught unprepared. The afflicted region became known as the "Dust Bowl."

By the mid-1930s, the drought had crippled countless farm families, and America had fallen into the Great Depression. Unable to pay their mortgages or invest in the kinds of industrial equipment now necessitated by commercial competition, many Dust Bowl farmers were forced to leave their land. Without any real employment prospects, thousands of families nonetheless traveled to California in hopes of finding new means of survival. But the farm country of California quickly became overcrowded with the migrant workers. Jobs and food were scarce, and the migrants faced prejudice and hostility from the Californians, who labeled them with the derisive epithet "Okie." These workers and their families lived in cramped, impoverished camps called "Hoovervilles," named after President Hoover, who was blamed for the problems that led to the Great Depression. Many of the residents of these camps starved to death, unable to find work.

2 ✿ JOHN STEINBECK

When Steinbeck decided to write a novel about the plight of migrant farm workers, he took his task very seriously. To prepare, he lived with an Oklahoma farm family and made the journey with them to California. When *The Grapes of Wrath* appeared, it soared to the top of the bestseller lists, selling nearly half a million copies. Although many Oklahomans and Californians reviled the book, considering Steinbeck's characters to be unflattering representations of their states' people, the large majority of readers and scholars praised the novel highly. The story of the Joad family captured a turbulent moment in American history and, in the words of critic Robert DeMott, "entered both the American consciousness and conscience." In 1940, the novel was awarded the Pulitzer Prize and adapted to the screen. Although Steinbeck went on to have a productive literary career and won the Novel Prize for Literature in 1962, none of his later books had the impact of *The Grapes of Wrath*. He died in 1968.

Today, readers of *The Grapes of Wrath* often find fault with its excessive sentimentality and generally flat characterizations, which seem at odds with Steinbeck's otherwise realistic style of writing. However, in writing his novel, Steinbeck attempted not only to describe the plight of migrant workers during the Depression but also to offer a pointed criticism of the policies that had caused that plight. In light of this goal, Steinbeck's characters often emerge as idealized archetypes or epic heroes; rather than using them to explore the individual human psyche, the author presents them as embodiments of universal ideals or struggles. Thus, the novel stands as a chronicle of the Depression and as a commentary on the economic and social system that gave rise to it.

Plot Overview

RELEASED FROM AN OKLAHOMA STATE PRISON after serving four years for a manslaughter conviction, Tom Joad makes his way back to his family's farm in Oklahoma. He meets Jim Casy, a former preacher who has given up his calling out of a belief that all life is holy—even the parts that are typically thought to be sinful—and that sacredness consists simply in endeavoring to be an equal among the people. Jim accompanies Tom to his home, only to find it—and all the surrounding farms—deserted. Muley Graves, an old neighbor, wanders by and tells the men that everyone has been "tractored" off the land. Most families, he says, including his own, have headed to California to look for work. The next morning, Tom and Jim set out for Tom's Uncle John's, where Muley assures them they will find the Joad clan. Upon arrival, Tom finds Ma and Pa Joad packing up the family's few possessions. Having seen handbills advertising fruit-picking jobs in California, they envision the trip to California as their only hope of getting their lives back on track.

The journey to California in a rickety used truck is long and arduous. Grampa Joad, a feisty old man who complains bitterly that he does not want to leave his land, dies on the road shortly after the family's departure. Dilapidated cars and trucks, loaded down with scrappy possessions, clog Highway 66: it seems the entire country is in flight to the Promised Land of California. The Joads meet Ivy and Sairy Wilson, a couple plagued with car trouble, and invite them to travel with the family. Sairy Wilson is sick and, near the California border, becomes unable to continue the journey.

As the Joads near California, they hear ominous rumors of a depleted job market. One migrant tells Pa that 20,000 people show up for every 800 jobs and that his own children have starved to death. Although the Joads press on, their first days in California prove tragic, as Granma Joad dies. The remaining family members move from one squalid camp to the next, looking in vain for work, struggling to find food, and trying desperately to hold their family together. Noah, the oldest of the Joad children, soon abandons the family, as does Connie, a young dreamer who is married to Tom's pregnant sister, Rose of Sharon.

The Joads meet with much hostility in California. The camps are overcrowded and full of starving migrants, who are often nasty to each other. The locals are fearful and angry at the flood of newcomers, whom they derisively label "Okies." Work is almost impossible to find or pays such a meager wage that a family's full day's work cannot buy a decent meal. Fearing an uprising, the large landowners do everything in their power to keep the migrants poor and dependent. While staying in a ramshackle camp known as a "Hooverville," Tom and several men get into a heated argument with a deputy sheriff over whether workers should organize into a union. When the argument turns violent, Tom knocks the sheriff unconscious and Jim Casy is blamed and arrested. Police officers arrive and announce their intention to burn the Hooverville to the ground.

A government-run camp proves much more hospitable to the Joads, and the family soon finds many friends and a bit of work. However, one day, while working at a pipe-laying job, Tom learns that the police are planning to stage a riot in the camp, which will allow them to shut down the facilities. By alerting and organizing the men in the camp, Tom helps to defuse the danger. Still, as pleasant as life in the government camp is, the Joads cannot survive without steady work, and they have to move on. They find employment picking fruit, but soon learn that they are earning a decent wage only because they have been hired to break a workers' strike. Tom runs into Jim Casy who, after being released from jail, has begun organizing workers; in the process, Casy has made many enemies among the landowners. When the police hunt him down and kill him in Tom's presence, Tom retaliates and kills a police officer.

Tom goes into hiding, while the family moves into a boxcar on a cotton farm. One day, Ruthie, the youngest Joad daughter, reveals to a girl in the camp that her brother has killed two men and is hiding nearby. Fearing for his safety, Ma Joad finds Tom and sends him away. Tom heads off to fulfill Jim's task of organizing the migrant workers. The end of the cotton season means the end of work, and word sweeps across the land that there are no jobs to be had for three months. Rains set in and flood the land. Rose of Sharon gives birth to a stillborn child, and Ma, desperate to get her family to safety from the floods, leads them to a dry barn not far away. Here, they find a young boy kneeling over his father, who is slowly starving to death. He has not eaten for days, giving whatever food he had to his son. Realizing that Rose of Sharon is now producing milk, Ma sends the others outside, so that her daughter can nurse the dying man.

CHARACTER LIST

Tom Joad   The novel's protagonist, and Ma and Pa Joad's favorite
son. Tom is good-natured and thoughtful and makes
do with what life hands him. Even though he killed a
man and has been separated from his family for four
years, he does not waste his time with regrets. He lives
fully for the present moment, which enables him to be a
great source of vitality for the Joad family. A wise guide
and fierce protector, Tom exhibits a moral certainty
throughout the novel that imbues him with strength
and resolve: he earns the awed respect of his family
members as well as the workers he later organizes
into unions.

Ma Joad   The mother of the Joad family. Ma is introduced as a
woman who knowingly and gladly fulfills her role as
"the citadel of the family." She is the healer of the
family's ills and the arbiter of its arguments, and her
ability to perform these tasks grows as the novel
progresses.

Pa Joad   Ma Joad's husband and Tom's father. Pa Joad is an
Oklahoma tenant farmer who has been evicted from
his farm. A plainspoken, good-hearted man, Pa directs
the effort to take the family to California. Once there,
unable to find work and increasingly desperate, Pa
finds himself looking to Ma Joad for strength and
leadership, though he sometimes feels ashamed of his
weaker position.

Jim Casy   A former preacher who gave up his ministry out of a
belief that all human experience is holy. Often the
moral voice of the novel, Casy articulates many of its
most important themes, among them the sanctity of the
people and the essential unity of all mankind. A

staunch friend of Tom Joad, Casy goes to prison in Tom's stead for a fight that erupts between laborers and the California police. He emerges a determined organizer of the migrant workers.

Rose of Sharon The oldest of Ma and Pa Joad's daughters, and Connie's wife. An impractical, petulant, and romantic young woman, Rose of Sharon begins the journey to California pregnant with her first child. She and Connie have grand notions of making a life for themselves in a city. The harsh realities of migrant life soon disabuse Rose of Sharon of these ideas, however. Her husband abandons her, and her child is born dead. By the end of the novel, she matures considerably, and possesses, the reader learns with surprise, something of her mother's indomitable spirit and grace.

Grampa Joad Tom Joad's grandfather. The founder of the Joad farm, Grampa is now old and infirm. Once possessed of a cruel and violent temper, Grampa's wickedness is now limited almost exclusively to his tongue. He delights in tormenting his wife and shocking others with sinful talk. Although his character serves largely to produce comical effect, he exhibits a very real and poignant connection to the land. The family is forced to drug him in order to get him to leave the homestead; removed from his natural element, however, Grampa soon dies.

Granma Joad Granma is a pious Christian, who loves casting hellfire and damnation in her husband's direction. Her health deteriorates quickly after Grandpa's death; she dies just after the family reaches California.

Al Joad om's younger brother, a sixteen-year-old boy obsessed with cars and girls. Al is vain and cocky but an extremely competent mechanic, and his expertise proves vital in bringing the Joads, as well as the Wilsons, to California. He idolizes Tom, but by the end of the novel he has become his own man. When he falls in love with a girl named Agnes Wainwright at a cotton plantation where they are working, he decides to stay with her rather than leaving with his family.

Ivy and Sairy Wilson A couple traveling to California whom the Joads meet on Highway 66, just before Grampa's death. The Wilsons lend the Joads their tent so that Grampa can have a comfortable place to die. The Joads return the couple's kindness by fixing their broken-down car. Hoping to make the trip easier, the two families combine forces, traveling together until Sairy Wilson's health forces her and Ivy to stop.

Connie Rose of Sharon's husband, Connie is an unrealistic dreamer who abandons the Joads after they reach California. This act of selfishness and immaturity surprises no one but his naïve wife.

Noah Joad Tom's older brother. Noah has been slightly deformed since his birth: Pa Joad had to perform the delivery and, panicking, tried to pull him out forcibly. Slow and quiet, Noah leaves his family behind at a stream near the California border, telling Tom that he feels his parents do not love him as much as they love the other children.

Uncle John Tom's uncle, who, years ago, refused to fetch a doctor for his pregnant wife when she complained of stomach pains. He has never forgiven himself for her death, and he often dwells heavily on the negligence he considers a sin.

Ruthie Joad The second and younger Joad daughter. Ruthie has a fiery relationship to her brother Winfield: the two are intensely dependent upon one another and fiercely competitive. When she brags to another child that her brother has killed two men, she inadvertently puts Tom's life in danger, forcing him to flee.

Winfield Joad At the age of ten, Winfield is the youngest of the Joad children. Ma worries for his well-being, fearing that without a proper home he will grow up to be wild and rootless.

Floyd Knowles The migrant worker who first inspires Tom and Casy to work for labor organization. Floyd's outspokenness sparks a scuffle with the police in which Casy is arrested.

Muley Graves One of the Joads' Oklahoma neighbors. When the bank evicts his family, Muley refuses to leave his land. Instead, he lets his wife and children move to California without him and stays behind to live outdoors. When he comes upon Tom at the abandoned Joad farm, he directs the young man to his Uncle John's.

Agnes Wainwright The daughter of the couple who shares the Joads' boxcar toward the end of the novel. Agnes becomes engaged to Al, who leaves his family in order to stay with her.

ANALYSIS OF MAJOR CHARACTERS

TOM JOAD

Tom begins the novel in possession of a practical sort of self-interest. Four years in prison, he claims, have molded him into someone who devotes his time and energies to the present moment. The future, which seems illusory and out of reach, does not concern him. He adopts this philosophy toward living not because he is selfish but as a means of coping: he fears that by putting his life in a context larger than the present day, he will drive himself mad with anger and helplessness. Of course, Tom, who exhibits a rare strength, thoughtfulness, and moral certainty, is destined for more than mere day-to-day survival. Tom undergoes the most significant transformation in the novel as he sheds this carpe diem (seize the day) philosophy for a commitment to bettering the future.

During their journey west, Tom assumes the role of Jim Casy's reluctant disciple. The former preacher emphasizes that a human being, when acting alone, can have little effect on the world, and that one can achieve wholeness only by devoting oneself to one's fellow human beings. The hardship and hostility faced by the Joad family on their journey west serve to convert Tom to Casy's teachings. By the time Tom and Casy reunite at the cotton plantation, Tom realizes that he cannot stand by as a silent witness to the world's injustices; he cannot work for his own family's well-being if it means taking bread from another family. At the plantation, Tom abandons the life of private thought that structures the lives of most of the novel's male characters—including Pa Joad and Uncle John—and sets out on a course of public action.

MA JOAD

A determined and loving woman, Ma Joad emerges as the family's center of strength over the course of the novel as Pa Joad gradually becomes less effective as a leader and provider. Regardless of how bleak circumstances become, Ma Joad meets every obstacle unflinchingly. Time and again, Ma displays a startling capacity to keep herself together—and to keep the family together—in the face of great turmoil. She may demonstrate this faculty best during the family's crossing of the California desert. Here, Ma suffers privately with the knowledge that Granma is dead, riding silently alongside her corpse so that the family can complete its treacherous journey. At the end of the episode, Ma's calm exterior cracks just slightly: she warns Tom not to touch her, saying that she can retain her calm only as long as he doesn't reach out to her. This ability to act decisively, and to act for the family's good, enables Ma to lead the Joads when Pa begins to falter and hesitate. Although she keeps her sorrows to herself, she is not an advocate of solitude. She consistently proves to be the novel's strongest supporter of family and togetherness. Indeed, the two tendencies are not in conflict but convene in a philosophy of selfless sacrifice. Ma articulates this best, perhaps, when she wordlessly directs her daughter to breast-feed the starving man in Chapter Thirty. With her indomitable nature, Ma Joad suggests that even the most horrible circumstances can be weathered with grace and dignity.

PA JOAD

Pa Joad is a good, thoughtful man, and he plans the family's trip to California with great care and consideration. The hardships faced by the Joads prove too great for him, however, and although he works hard to maintain his role as head of the family, he complains of muddled thoughts and finds himself in frequent quandaries. Until the very end, Pa exhibits a commitment to protecting his family. His determination to erect a dam is a moving testament to his love and singleness of purpose. When his efforts begin to fall short, however, Pa despairs. In California, his inability to find work forces him to retreat helplessly into his own thoughts. As a result, he becomes less and less effective in his role as family leader, and Ma points this out directly. Upon leaving the Weedpatch camp, she boldly criticizes him for losing sight of his responsibility to support the family. By the end of the novel, further diminished by the failed attempt to prevent the family's shelter from flooding, he follows Ma as blindly and helplessly as a child. Pa's gradual breakdown serves as a sharp reminder that hardship does not always "build character." Though the challenges of the Joads' journey serve to strengthen Ma, Tom, and even Rose of Sharon, they weaken and eventually paralyze Pa.

JIM CASY

Steinbeck employs Jim Casy to articulate some of the novel's major themes. Most notably, the ex-preacher redefines the concept of holiness, suggesting that the most divine aspect of human experience is to be found on earth, among one's fellow humans, rather than amid the clouds. As a radical philosopher, a motivator and unifier of men, and a martyr, Casy assumes a role akin to that of Jesus Christ—with whom he also shares his initials. Casy begins the novel uncertain of how to use his talents as a speaker and spiritual healer if not as the leader of a religious congregation. By the end of the novel, he has learned to apply them to his task of organizing the migrant workers. Indeed, Casy comes to believe so strongly in his mission to save the suffering laborers that he willingly gives his life for it. Casy's teachings prompt the novel's most dramatic character development, by catalyzing Tom Joad's transformation into a social activist and man of the people.

ROSE OF SHARON

In creating the character of Rose of Sharon, Steinbeck relies heavily on stereotypes. We read that pregnancy has transformed the girl from a "hoyden"—a high-spirited and saucy girl—into a secretive and mysterious woman. Time and again, Steinbeck alludes to the girl's silent self-containment and her impenetrable smile. This portrayal of pregnancy may initially seem to bespeak a romanticism out of keeping with Steinbeck's characteristic realism. However, Steinbeck uses such seemingly trite details to prepare Rose of Sharon for the dramatic role she plays at the end of the novel. When she meets the starving man in the barn, she becomes saintly, otherworldly. Her capacity to sustain life, paired with her suffering and grief for her dead child, liken her to the Virgin Mother and suggest that there is hope to be found even in the bleakest of circumstances.

Themes, Motifs & Symbols

Themes

Themes are the fundamental and often universal ideas explored in a literary work.

Man's Inhumanity to Man

Steinbeck consistently and woefully points to the fact that the migrants' great suffering is caused not by bad weather or mere misfortune but by their fellow human beings. Historical, social, and economic circumstances separate people into rich and poor, landowner and tenant, and the people in the dominant roles struggle viciously to preserve their positions. In his brief history of California in Chapter Nineteen, Steinbeck portrays the state as the product of land-hungry squatters who took the land from Mexicans and, by working it and making it produce, rendered it their own. Now, generations later, the California landowners see this historical example as a threat, since they believe that the influx of migrant farmers might cause history to repeat itself. In order to protect themselves from such danger, the landowners create a system in which the migrants are treated like animals, shuffled from one filthy roadside camp to the next, denied livable wages, and forced to turn against their brethren simply to survive. The novel draws a simple line through the population—one that divides the privileged from the poor—and identifies that division as the primary source of evil and suffering in the world.

The Saving Power of Family and Fellowship

The Grapes of Wrath chronicles the story of two "families": the Joads and the collective body of migrant workers. Although the Joads are joined by blood, the text argues that it is not their genetics but their loyalty and commitment to one another that establishes their true kinship. In the migrant lifestyle portrayed in the book, the biological family unit, lacking a home to define its boundaries, quickly becomes a thing of the past, as life on the road demands that new connections and new kinships be formed. The reader witnesses this phenomenon at work when the Joads meet the Wilsons. In a remarkably short time, the two groups merge into one, sharing one another's hardships and committing to one another's survival. This merging takes place among the migrant community in general as well: "twenty families became one family, the children were the children of all. The loss of home became one loss, and the golden time in the West was one dream." In the face of adversity, the livelihood of the migrants depends upon their union. As Tom eventually realizes, "his" people are *all* people.

THE DIGNITY OF WRATH

The Joads stand as exemplary figures in their refusal to be broken by the circumstances that conspire against them. At every turn, Steinbeck seems intent on showing their dignity and honor; he emphasizes the importance of maintaining self-respect in order to survive spiritually. Nowhere is this more evident than at the end of the novel. The Joads have suffered incomparable losses: Noah, Connie, and Tom have left the family; Rose of Sharon gives birth to a stillborn baby; the family possesses neither food nor promise of work. Yet it is at this moment (Chapter Thirty) that the family manages to rise above hardship to perform an act of unsurpassed kindness and generosity for the starving man, showing that the Joads have not lost their sense of the value of human life.

Steinbeck makes a clear connection in his novel between dignity and rage. As long as people maintain a sense of injustice—a sense of anger against those who seek to undercut their pride in themselves—they will never lose their dignity. This notion receives particular reinforcement in Steinbeck's images of the festering grapes of wrath (Chapter Twenty-Five), and in the last of the short, expository chapters (Chapter Twenty-Nine), in which the worker women, watching their husbands and brothers and sons, know that these men will remain strong "as long as fear [can] turn to wrath." The women's certainty is based on their understanding that the men's wrath bespeaks their healthy sense of self-respect.

THE MULTIPLYING EFFECTS OF SELFISHNESS AND ALTRUISM

According to Steinbeck, many of the evils that plague the Joad family and the migrants stem from selfishness. Simple self-interest motivates the landowners and businessmen to sustain a system that sinks thousands of families into poverty. In contrast to and in conflict with this policy of selfishness stands the migrants' behavior toward one another. Aware that their livelihood and survival depend upon their devotion to the collective good, the migrants unite—sharing their dreams as well as their burdens—in order to survive. Throughout the novel, Steinbeck constantly emphasizes self-interest and altruism as equal and opposite powers, evenly matched in their conflict with each other. In Chapters Thirteen and Fifteen, for example, Steinbeck presents both greed and generosity as self-perpetuating, following cyclical dynamics. In Chapter Thirteen, we learn that corporate gas companies have preyed upon the gas station attendant that the Joads meet. The attendant, in turn, insults the Joads and hesitates to help them. Then, after a brief expository chapter, the Joads immediately happen upon an instance of kindness as similarly self-propagating: Mae, a waitress, sells bread and sweets to a man and his sons for drastically reduced prices. Some truckers at the coffee shop see this interchange and leave Mae an extra-large tip.

MOTIFS

Motifs are recurring structures, contrasts, or literary devices that can help to develop and inform the text's major themes.

IMPROVISED LEADERSHIP STRUCTURES

When the novel begins, the Joad family relies on a traditional family structure in which the men make the decisions and the women obediently do as they are told. So invested are they in these roles that they continue to honor Grampa as the head of the family, even though he has outlived his ability to act as a sound leader. As the Joads journey west and try to make a living in California, however, the family dynamic changes drastically. Discouraged and defeated by his mounting failures, Pa withdraws from his role as leader and spends his days tangled in thought. In his stead, Ma assumes the responsibility of making decisions for the family. At first, this shocks Pa, who, at one point, lamely threatens to beat her into her so-called proper place. The threat is empty, however, and the entire family knows it. By the end of the novel, the family structure has undergone a revolution, in which the woman figure, traditionally powerless, has taken control, while the male figure, traditionally in the leadership role, has retreated. This revolution parallels a similar upheaval in the larger economic hierarchies in the outside world. Thus, the workers at the Weedpatch camp govern themselves according to their own rules and share tasks in accordance with notions of fairness and equality rather than power-hungry ambition or love of authority.

SYMBOLS

Symbols are objects, characters, figures, or colors used to represent abstract ideas or concepts.

ROSE OF SHARON'S PREGNANCY

Rose of Sharon's pregnancy holds the promise of a new beginning. When she delivers a stillborn baby, that promise seems broken. But rather than slipping into despair, the family moves boldly and gracefully forward, and the novel ends on a surprising (albeit unsettling) note of hope. In the last few pages of his book, Steinbeck employs many symbols, a number of which refer directly to episodes in the Bible. The way in which Uncle John disposes of the child's corpse recalls Moses being sent down the Nile. The image suggests that the family, like the Hebrews in Egypt, will be delivered from the slavery of its present circumstances.

THE DEATH OF THE JOADS' DOG

When the Joads stop for gas not long after they begin their trip west, they are met by a hostile station attendant, who accuses them of being beggars and vagrants. While there, a fancy roadster runs down their dog and leaves it for dead in the middle of the road. The gruesome death constitutes the first of many symbols foreshadowing the tragedies that await the family.

Summary & Analysis

Chapters One–Three

Summary: Chapter One
The cornfields of Oklahoma shrivel and fade in a long summer drought. Thick clouds of dust fill the skies, and the farmers tie handkerchiefs over their noses and mouths. At night, the dust blocks out the stars and creeps in through cracks in the farmhouses. During the day the farmers have nothing to do but stare dazedly at their dying crops, wondering how their families will survive. Their wives and children watch them in turn, fearful that the disaster will break the men and leave the families destitute. They know that no misfortune will be too great to bear as long as their men remain "whole."

Summary: Chapter Two
Into this desolate country enters Tom Joad, newly released from the McAlester State Penitentiary, where he served four years on a manslaughter conviction. Dressed in a cheap new suit, Tom hitches a ride with a trucker he meets at a roadside restaurant. The trucker's vehicle carries a "No Riders" sign, but Tom asks the trucker to be a "good guy" even if "some rich bastard makes him carry a sticker." As they travel down the road, the driver asks Tom about himself, and Tom explains that he is returning to his father's farm. The driver is surprised that the Joads have not been driven off their property by a "cat," a large tractor sent by landowners and bankers to force poor farmers off the land. The driver reports that much has changed during Tom's absence: great numbers of families have been "tractored out" of their small farms. The driver fears that Tom has taken offense at his questions and assures him that he's not a man to stick his nose in other folks' business. The loneliness of life on the road, he confides in Tom, can wear a man down. Tom senses the man looking him over, noticing his clothes, and admits that he has just been released from prison. The driver assures Tom that such news does not bother him. Tom laughs, telling the driver that he now has a story to tell "in every joint from here to Texola." The truck comes to a stop at the road leading to the Joads' farm, and Tom gets out.

SUMMARY: CHAPTER THREE

In the summer heat, a turtle plods across the baking highway. A woman careens her car aside to avoid hitting the turtle, but a young man veers his truck straight at the turtle, trying to run it over. He nicks the edge of the turtle's shell, flipping it off the highway and onto its back. Legs jerking in the air, the turtle struggles to flip itself back over. Eventually it succeeds and continues trudging on its way.

ANALYSIS: CHAPTERS ONE–THREE

The Grapes of Wrath derives its epic scope from the way that Steinbeck uses the story of the Joad family to portray the plight of thousands of Dust Bowl farmers. The structure of the novel reflects this dual commitment: Steinbeck tracks the Joad family with long narrative chapters but alternates these sections with short, lyrical vignettes, capturing the westward movement of migrant farmers in the 1930s as they flee drought and industry.

This structure enables Steinbeck to use many different writing styles. The short (usually odd-numbered) chapters use highly stylized, poetic language to explore the social, economic, and historical factors that forced the great migration. Steinbeck's first description of the land is almost biblical in its simplicity, grandeur, and repetition: "The surface of the earth crusted, a thin hard crust, and as the sky became pale, so the earth became pale, pink in the red country and white in the gray country." The chapters devoted to the Joads' story are noteworthy for their remarkably realistic evocation of life and language among Oklahoma sharecroppers. Here Steinbeck displays his talent for rich, naturalistic narration. (Naturalism is a school of writing favoring realistic representations of human life and natural, as opposed to supernatural or spiritual, explanations for social phenomena.) Expertly rendered details place the reader squarely and immediately in the book's setting, quickly drawing us in after an interlude of more distanced poetics. Steinbeck also skillfully captures the colorful, rough dialogue of his folk heroes—"You had that big nose goin' over me like a sheep in a vegetable patch," Tom says to the truck driver in Chapter Two—thus bringing them to life. By employing a wide range of styles, Steinbeck achieves what he called a "symphony in composition, in movement, in tone and scope."

The opening of the novel also establishes several of the novel's dominant themes. Steinbeck dedicates the first and third chapters, respectively, to a historical and symbolic description of the Dust

Bowl tragedy. While Chapter One paints an impressionistic picture of the Oklahoma farms as they wither and die, Chapter Three presents a symbolic depiction of the farmers' plights in the turtle that struggles to cross the road. Both chapters share a particularly dark vision of the world. As the relentless weather of Chapter One and the mean-spirited driver of Chapter Three represent, the universe is full of obstacles that fill life with hardship and danger. Like the turtle that trudges across the road, the Joad family will be called upon, time and again, to fight the malicious forces—drought, industry, human jealousy and fear—that seek to overturn it.

CHAPTERS FOUR–SIX

SUMMARY: CHAPTER FOUR

As Tom plods along the dusty road, he notices a turtle. He picks it up, wraps it in his coat, and takes it with him. Continuing on, he notices a tattered man sitting under a tree. The man recognizes him and introduces himself as Jim Casy, the preacher in Tom's church when Tom was a boy. Casy says that he baptized Tom, but Tom was too busy pulling a girl's pigtails to have taken much interest in the event. Tom gives the old preacher a drink from his flask of liquor, and Casy tells Tom how he decided to stop preaching. He admits that he had a habit of taking girls "out in the grass" after prayer meetings and tells Tom that he was conflicted for some time, not knowing how to reconcile his sexual appetites with his responsibility for these young women's souls. Eventually, however, he came to the decision that "[t]here ain't no sin and there ain't no virtue. There's just stuff people do. It's all part of the same thing." No longer convinced that human pleasures run counter to a divine plan, Casy believes that the human spirit *is* the Holy Spirit.

Casy asks Tom about his father, and Tom replies that he hasn't seen or heard from him in years. Tom divulges the crime that landed him in prison, explaining that he and another man, both drunk, got into a fight; the man stabbed Tom, and Tom killed him with a nearby shovel. He describes life in prison, where he received regular meals and baths. Despite this good treatment, however, he notes that the lack of women made life hard. As Tom prepares to continue toward his home, Casy asks if he can come along. Tom welcomes him, and comments that the Joads always thought highly of their preacher. They walk to the farm, but upon arriving at the site, they realize it has been deserted.

SUMMARY: CHAPTER FIVE

The landowners and the banks, unable to make high profits from tenant farming, evict the farmers from the land. (Tenant farming is an agricultural system in which farmers live on the property of a landowner and share in the profits.) Some of the property owners are cruel, some are kind, but they all deliver the same news: the farmers must leave. The farmers protest, complaining that they have nowhere to go. The owners suggest they go to California, where there is work to be done. Tractors arrive on the land, with orders to plow the property, crushing anything in their paths—including, if necessary, the farmhouse. The tractors are often driven by the farmers' neighbors, who explain that their own families have nothing to eat and that the banks pay several dollars a day. Livid, the displaced farmers yearn to fight back, but the banks are so faceless, impersonal, and inhuman that they cannot be fought against.

SUMMARY: CHAPTER SIX

Tom and Casy find the Joad homestead strangely untouched, other than a section of the farmhouse that has been crushed. The presence of usable materials and tools on the premises, apparently unscavenged, signifies to Tom that the neighbors, too, must have deserted their farms. Tom and Casy see Muley Graves walking toward them. He reports that the Joads have moved in with Tom's Uncle John. The entire family has gone to work picking cotton in hopes of earning enough money to buy a car and make the journey to California. Muley explains haltingly that a large company has bought all the land in the area and evicted the tenant farmers in order to cut labor costs. When Tom asks if he can stay at Muley's place for the night, Muley explains that he, too, has lost his land and that his family has already departed for California. Hearing this, Casy criticizes Muley's decision to stay behind: "You shouldn't of broke up the fambly." Hungry, the men share the rabbits Muley caught hunting. After dinner, the headlights of a police car sweep across the land. Afraid that they will be arrested for trespassing, they hide, though Tom balks at the idea of hiding from the police on his own farm. Muley takes them to a cave where he sleeps. Tom sleeps in the open air outside the cave, but Casy says that he cannot sleep: his mind is too burdened with what the men have learned.

ANALYSIS: CHAPTERS FOUR–SIX

As the novel unfolds, the short, descriptive chapters emerge like a series of thesis statements on the conditions of life in the Dust Bowl.

The chapters recounting the story of the Joad clan can be seen as illustrations of or evidence for the claims made in the shorter chapters. In Chapter Five, Steinbeck sets forth an argument strongly supportive of tenant farmers. Notably, however, he does not directly vilify the landowners and bank representatives as they turn the tenant farmers off their land. He asserts that the economic system makes everyone a victim—rich and poor, privileged and disenfranchised. All are caught "in something larger than themselves." It is this larger monster that has created the divides between the victims, stratified them, and turned the upper strata against the lower. Still, Steinbeck does not portray in detail the personal difficulties of the men who evict the farmers, nor of the conflicted neighbors who plow down their farms. His sympathies clearly lie with the farmers, and his descriptive eye follows these sympathies. Correspondingly, it is with these families that the reader comes to identify.

The Grapes of Wrath openly and without apology declares its stance on the events it portrays. This sense of commitment and candor stems from Steinbeck's method of characterization, as well as from his insistence on setting up the Joads and their clan as models of moral virtue. Although Tom Joad has spent four years in prison, he soon emerges as a kind of moral authority in the book. A straight-talking man, Tom begins his trek home by putting a nosy truck driver in his place—having served the lawful punishment for his crime, he owns up to his past without indulging in regret or shame. His deeply thoughtful disposition, truthful speech, and gestures of generosity endear him to the reader, as well as those around him. He will soon emerge as a leader among his people. His leadership ability stems also from his sense of confidence and sureness of purpose. Tom admits to Casy that if he found himself in a situation similar to the one that landed him in jail, he would behave no differently now. This statement does not convey pride or vanity but a capacity to know and be honest with himself, as well as a steady resolve.

If Tom Joad emerges as the novel's moral consciousness, then Jim Casy emerges as its moral mouthpiece. Although he claims he has lost his calling as a preacher, Casy remains a great talker, and he rarely declines an opportunity to make a speech. At many points, Steinbeck uses him to voice the novel's themes. Here, for instance, Casy describes the route by which he left the pulpit. After several sexual affairs with young women in his congregation, Casy realized that the immediate pleasures of human life were more important than lofty concepts of theological virtue. He decided that he did not need to be a preacher to experience holiness: simply being an equal among one's fellow human beings was sacred in its own way. This philosophy is lived out by the Joads, who soon discover that open, sincere fellowship with others is more precious than any longed-for commodity. Casy further emphasizes the virtues of companionship when he chastises Muley Graves. The man has allowed his family to leave for California without him, for the sake of practicality, but Casy believes that togetherness and cooperation should always take precedence over practicality.

CHAPTERS SEVEN–NINE

SUMMARY: CHAPTER SEVEN

The narrator assumes the voice of a used-car salesman explaining to his employees how to cheat the departing families. The great westward exodus has created a huge demand for automobiles, and dusty used-car lots spring up throughout the area. Crooked salesmen sell the departing families whatever broken-down vehicles they can find. The salesmen fill engines with sawdust to conceal noisy transmissions and replace good batteries with cracked ones before they deliver the cars. The tenant farmers, desperate to move and with little knowledge of cars, willingly pay the skyrocketing prices, much to the salesmen's delight.

SUMMARY: CHAPTER EIGHT

*[W]hen they're all workin' together, not one fella for
another fella, but one fella kind of harnessed to the
whole shebang . . . that's holy.*

(*See* QUOTATIONS, *p.* 43)

As the men travel to Uncle John's, Tom relates a story about his curious uncle. Years ago, John dismissed his wife's complaints of a stomachache and refused to hire a doctor for her. When she subsequently died, John was unable to deal with the loss. Tom describes his constant acts of generosity, handing out candy to children or delivering a sack of meal to a neighbor, as if trying to make up for his one fatal instance of stinginess. Despite his efforts, John remains unable to console himself.

At Uncle John's house, Tom is reunited with his family. He comes upon his father, Pa Joad, piling the family's belongings outside. Neither Pa nor Ma Joad recognizes Tom at first, and, until he explains that he has been paroled from prison, both fear that he has broken out illegally. They tell him that they are about to leave for California. Ma Joad worries that life in prison may have driven Tom insane: she knew the mother of a gangster, "Purty Boy Floyd," who went "mean-mad" in prison. Tom assures his mother that he lacks the stubborn pride of those who find prison a devastating insult. "I let stuff run off'n me," he says. Tom also reunites with fiery old Grampa and Granma Joad, and with his withdrawn and slow-moving brother Noah.

At breakfast, Granma, who is devoutly religious, insists that Casy say a prayer, even though he tells them he no longer preaches. Instead of a traditional prayer, he shares his realization that mankind is holy in itself. The Joads do not begin the meal, however, until he follows the speech with an "amen." Pa Joad shows Tom the truck he has bought for the family and says that Tom's younger brother Al, who knows a bit about cars, helped him pick it out. When sixteen-year-old Al arrives at the house, his admiration and respect for Tom is clear. Tom learns that his two youngest siblings, Ruthie and Winfield, are in town with Uncle John. Rose of Sharon, another sister, has married Connie, a boy from a neighboring farm, and is expecting a child.

Summary: Chapter Nine

The narrator shifts focus from the Joads to describe how the tenant farmers in general prepare for the journey to California. For much of the chapter, the narrator assumes the voice of typical tenant farmers, expressing what their possessions and memories of their homes mean to them. The farmers are forced to pawn most of their belongings, both to raise money for the trip and simply because they cannot take them on the road. In the frenzied buying and selling that follows, the farmers have no choice but to deal with brokers who pay outrageously low prices, knowing that the farmers are in no position to bargain. Disappointed, the farmers return to their wives and report that they have sold most of their property for a pocketful of change. The wives linger over objects with sentimental value, but everything must be sold or destroyed before the families can leave for California.

Analysis: Chapters Seven–Nine

Chapter Eight introduces us to the Joad family. Steinbeck sketches a good number of memorable characters in the space of a single chapter. Pa appears as a competent, fair-minded, and good-hearted head of the family, leading the Joads in their journeys, while Ma emerges as the family's "citadel," anchoring them and keeping them safe. Steinbeck does not render the Joads as particularly complex characters. Instead, each family member tends to possess one or two exaggerated, distinguishing characteristics. Grampa, for instance, is mischievous and ornery; Granma is excessively pious; Al, a typically cocky teenaged boy, is obsessed with cars and girls.

Some readers find fault with Steinbeck's method of characterization, which they criticize as unsophisticated and sentimental, but this criticism may be unfair. It is true that the Joads are not shown as having the kind of complex psychological lives that mark many great literary characters. Their desires are simple and clearly stated, and the obstacles to their desires are plainly identified by both the novel and themselves. However, it is in the nature of an epic to portray heroic, boldly drawn figures—figures who embody national ideals or universal struggles. Steinbeck succeeds in crafting the Joads into heroes worthy of an epic. Their goodness, conviction, and moral certainty stand in sharp contrast to their material circumstances.

The short chapters that bookend the introduction of the Joad family develop one of the book's major themes. The narrative's indictment of the crooked car salesmen and pawnbrokers illustrates man's inhumanity to man, a force against which the Joads struggle. Time and again, those in positions of power seek to take advantage of those below them. Even when giving up a portion of land might save a family, the privileged refuse to imperil their wealth. Later in the novel, there is nothing that the California landowners fear as much as relinquishing their precious land to the needy farmers. This behavior contradicts Jim Casy's belief that men must act for the good of all men. In *The Grapes of Wrath*, moral order depends upon this kind of selflessness and charity. Without these virtues, the text suggests, there is no hope for a livable world. As one farmer warns the corrupt pawnbroker who robs him of his possessions: "[Y]ou cut us down, and soon you will be cut down and there'll be none of us to save you."

CHAPTERS TEN–TWELVE

SUMMARY: CHAPTER TEN

Tom and Ma Joad discuss California. Ma worries about what they will find there but trusts that the handbill she read that advertised work was accurate and that California will be a wonderful place.

Grampa agrees, boasting that when he arrives there he will fill his mouth with grapes and let the juices run down his chin. Pa Joad has gone to town to sell off some of the family's possessions. Now he returns discouraged, having earned a mere eighteen dollars. The Joads hold a council during which it is decided that Casy may travel with them to California; then they set about packing to leave. Casy helps Ma Joad salt the meat. Despite her protests that salting is women's work, Casy convinces her that the amount of work facing them renders such preoccupations invalid. Rose of Sharon and Connie arrive, and the family piles onto the truck. When the time comes to leave, Muley Graves bids the family good-bye, but Grampa suddenly wants to stay. He claims that he aims to live off the land like Muley and continues to protest loudly until the Joads lace his coffee with sleeping medicine. Once the old man is asleep, the family loads him onto the truck and begins the long journey west.

SUMMARY: CHAPTER ELEVEN
When the farmers leave their land, the land becomes vacant. The narrator explains that even though men continue to work the land, these men have no real connection to their work. Possessed of little knowledge or skill, these corporate farm workers come to the farm during the day, drive a tractor over it, and leave to go home. Such a separation between work and life causes men to lose wonder for their work and for the land. The farmer's "deep understanding" of the land and his relationship to it cease to be. The empty farmhouses are quickly invaded by animals and begin to crumble in the dust and the wind.

SUMMARY: CHAPTER TWELVE
Long lines of cars creep down Highway 66, full of tenant farmers making their way to California. The narrator again assumes the voices of typical farmers, expressing their worries about their vehicles and the dangers of the journey. When the farmers stop to buy parts for their cars, salesmen try to cheat them. The farmers struggle to make it from service station to service station, fleeing from the desolation they have left behind. They are met with hostility and suspicion. People inquire about their journey, claiming that the country is not large enough to support everybody's needs and suggesting that they go back to where they came from. Still, one finds rare instances of hope and beauty, such as the stranded family that possesses only a trailer—no motor to pull it—and waits by the side of the road for lifts. They make it to California "in two jumps,"

proving that "strange things happen . . . some bitterly cruel and some so beautiful that faith is refired forever."

ANALYSIS: CHAPTERS TEN–TWELVE

In these chapters, Steinbeck continues to develop his picture of the farmers' world, with flashes of the desolate farms they flee, as well as of the many adverse circumstances that await them. Steinbeck suggests that the hardships the families face stem from more than harsh weather conditions or simple misfortune. Human beings, acting with calculated greed, are responsible for much of their sorrow. Such selfishness separates people from one another, disabling the kind of unity and brotherhood that Casy deems holy. It creates an ugly animosity that pits man against man, as is clear in Chapter Twelve, when a gas station attendant suggests that California is becoming overcrowded with migrants. When a farmer notes that surely California is a large enough state to support everyone, the attendant cynically replies, "There ain't room enough for you an' me, for your kind an' my kind, for rich and poor together all in one country."

This factionalism not only divides men from their brethren, it also divides men from the land. Steinbeck identifies greed and covetousness as the central cause of the tenant farmers' dislocation from the ground they have always known. The corporate farmers who replace the old families possess the same acquisitive mind-set as their employers. Interested only in getting their work done quickly and leaving with a paycheck, they treat the land with hostility, as an affliction rather than a home, and put heavy machinery between themselves and the fields.

Both Muley Graves and Grampa Joad represent the human reluctance to be separated from one's land. Both men locate their roots in the Oklahoma soil and both are willing to abandon their families in order to maintain this connection. Neither Muley nor Grampa Joad can imagine who he would be beyond the boundaries that, until now, have shaped and defined him. In their scheme to prevent Grampa from staying, the Joads engage in blatant dishonesty, yet their intentions are good. For the Joads mean to sever one kind of connection in favor of another, abandoning the land to keep the family together. They believe in the ability of human connections to sustain their grandfather's life and spirit.

As the Joads depart, their interactions speak further to their common belief in the importance of family and the family structure.

Men lead—even if, as in Grampa's case, their guidance is merely ceremonial—whereas women follow. It is important to note this structure now, for once the family is on the road, this traditional power dynamic shifts. This process is prefigured in Casy's insistence that he help Ma Joad salt the meat. Faced with dauntingly difficult work, the group can no longer cling to gender-based divisions of labor.

Thus, while economic adversity may frequently drive divisions between people, it can also serve to erase divisions, to emphasize everyone's common humanity. Steinbeck's text insists that the hardships of the road, while often creating ugliness, can also yield unexpected beauty. A single instance of charity or kindness emerges as an oasis of moral nobility, both testifying to and renewing the strength of the human spirit. Although the Joads declare the family's goal to be their arrival in California, it is these rare and serendipitous places along the road—in which hope is confirmed despite life's atrocities—that constitute the Joads' true destination.

CHAPTERS THIRTEEN–FIFTEEN

SUMMARY: CHAPTER THIRTEEN

Al skillfully guides the Joads' truck along Route 66, listening carefully to the engine for any trouble that might cause a breakdown. He asks Ma if she fears that California will not live up to their expectations, and she wisely says that she cannot account for what might be; she can only account for what is. They stop at a service station, where Al argues with an attendant who insinuates that the family has no money to pay for gas. The attendant laments that most of his customers have nothing and often stop to beg for the fuel. He explains that all the fancy new cars stop at the yellow-painted company stations in town. Although the man has attempted to paint his pumps yellow in imitation of the fancier stations, the underlying decrepitude of the place shows through. While the family drinks water and rests, their dog is hit by a car, and Rose of Sharon becomes frightened, worrying that witnessing something so gruesome will harm her baby. The attendant agrees to bury the dog, and the Joads continue on their way. They pass through Oklahoma City, a larger city than the family has ever seen. The sights and sounds of the place embarrass and frighten Ruthie and Winfield, while Rose of Sharon and Connie burst into giggles at the fashions they see worn for the first time. At the end of a day's travel, the family camps along the roadside and meets Ivy Wilson and his wife, Sairy, whose car has broken down. Grampa is sick, and the Wilsons offer him their tent for a rest, but before long the old man suffers a stroke and dies. The Joads improvise a funeral and bury their grandfather, despite the fact that it is against the law. Later, they convince the Wilsons that both groups would benefit from traveling together to California, and the Wilsons agree.

SUMMARY: CHAPTER FOURTEEN

The last clear definite function of man—muscles aching to work, minds aching to create beyond the single need—this is man.

(See QUOTATIONS, p. 43)

People who live in the West do not understand what has happened in Oklahoma and the Midwest. What began as a thin trickle of migrant farmers has become a flood. Families camp next to the road, and every ditch has become a settlement. Amid the deluge of poor farmers, the citizens of the western states are frightened and on edge. They fear that the dislocated farmers will come together; that the weak, when united, will become strong—strong enough, perhaps, to stage a revolt.

SUMMARY: CHAPTER FIFTEEN

A waitress named Mae and a cook named Al work at a coffee shop on Route 66. Mae watches the many cars pass by, hoping that truckers will stop, for they leave the biggest tips. One day, two truckers with whom Mae is friendly drop in for a piece of pie. They discuss the westward migration, and Mae reports that the farmers are rumored to be thieves. Just then, a tattered man and his two boys enter, asking if they can buy a loaf of bread for a dime. Mae brushes them off. She reminds the man that she is not running a grocery store, and that even if she did sell him a loaf of bread she would have to charge fifteen cents. From behind the counter, Al growls at Mae to give the man some bread, and she finally softens. Then she notices the two boys looking longingly at some nickel candy, and she sells their father two pieces for a penny. The truckers, witnessing this scene, leave Mae an extra-large tip.

ANALYSIS: CHAPTERS THIRTEEN–FIFTEEN

As the Joads set out for California, the second phase of the novel begins: their dramatic journey west. Almost immediately, the Joads are exposed to the very hardships that Steinbeck describes in the alternating expository chapters that chronicle the great migration as a whole; the account of the family provides a close-up on the larger picture. Thus, in Chapter Thirteen, at the gas station, the family encounters the hostility and suspicion described in Chapters Twelve, Fourteen, and Fifteen. The attendant unfairly pegs the Joads as vagrants and seems sure that they have come to beg gas from him. As Al's reaction makes clear, this accusation comes as a great insult to self-reliant people with a strong sense of dignity. The apologetic attendant confides in the Joads that his livelihood has been endangered by the fancy corporate service stations. He fears that he, like the poor tenant farmers, will soon be forced to find another way to make his living. Steinbeck is far from subtle in identifying capitalism and corporate interests as a source of great human tragedy, a form of "ritualized thievery." Corporate gas companies have preyed upon the attendant; the attendant, in turn, insults the Joads and is initially loath to offer them help. The system in force here works according to a vicious cycle, a cycle that perpetuates greed as a method of sheer survival.

These rather bleak observations cast a pall over the Joads' journey and point to even darker clouds on the horizon. Soon after arriving at the gas station, the Joads' dog is struck by a car. The dog's gruesome death stands as a symbol of the difficulties that await the family—difficulties that begin as soon as the family camps for the night. Before the family has been gone a full day, Grampa suffers a stroke and dies. Because Grampa was, at one point, the most enthusiastic proponent of the trip, dreaming of the day he would arrive in California and crush fat bunches of vine-ripened grapes in his mouth, his death foreshadows the harsh realities that await the family in the so-called Promised Land. With Grampa, something of the family's hope dies too.

Still, even in this forlorn world, opportunities to display kindness, virtue, and generosity exist. In this section, the narrator's statement from the end of Chapter Twelve is validated: there will be instances both of bitter cruelty and life-affirming beauty. The story of Mae, in its simplistic illustration of morality and virtue, functions almost like a parable, and considerably lightens the tone of these chapters. The lesson Mae learns is a simple one: compassion and generosity are rewarded in the world. Thus, although greed may be self-perpetuating, as the earlier chapters insist, so is kindness. The entrance of the Wilsons into the story also introduces a hopeful tone: by cooperating and looking after their communal interests, the families find a strength that they lack on their own.

CHAPTERS SIXTEEN–EIGHTEEN

SUMMARY: CHAPTER SIXTEEN

The Joad and Wilson families travel for two days. On the third day, they settle into a new routine whereby "the highway became their home and movement their medium of expression." Rose of Sharon declares that when they arrive in California, she and Connie plan to live in town, where Connie can study at night in preparation for managing his own store. This worries Ma Joad, who balks at any idea of splitting up the family. The Wilsons' car breaks down again. Tom and Casy offer to stay behind to repair it, but Ma refuses to go on without them. Instead, the whole group waits while Al and Tom go into town to find parts at a local car lot. The brothers find the needed part, and spend some time talking to the bitter, one-eyed attendant. The man complains tearfully of the injustices of his job. Tom urges him to pull himself together. At the crowded camp that night, Pa Joad tells a man that he is traveling to look for work in California. The man laughs at him, saying that there is no work in California, despite what the handbills promise. Wealthy farmers, the man reports, may need 800 workers, but they print 5000 handbills, which are seen by 20,000 people. The man says that his wife and children starved to death because he took them to find work in California. This worries Pa, but Casy tells him that the Joads may have a different experience than this man did.

SUMMARY: CHAPTER SEVENTEEN

As masses of cars travel together and camp along the highway, little communities spring up among the migrant farmers: "twenty families became one family." The communities create their own rules of conduct and their own means of enforcement. The lives of the farmers change drastically. They are no longer farmers but "migrant men."

SUMMARY: CHAPTER EIGHTEEN

After traveling through the mountains of New Mexico and the Arizona desert, the Joads and Wilsons arrive in California. They still face a great obstacle, however, as the desert lies between them and the lush valleys they have been expecting. The men find a river and go bathing. There, they meet a father and son who are returning from California because they have been unable to make a living. The man cautions the Joads about what awaits them there: the open hostility of people who derisively call them "Okies" and the wastefulness of ranchers with "a million acres."

Despite these warnings, the Joads decide to continue on, and to finish the journey that night. Noah decides to stay behind, saying he will live off fish from the river. He claims that his absence will not really hurt the family, for although his parents treat him with kindness, they really do not love him deeply. Tom tries in vain to convince him otherwise. Granma, whose health has deteriorated since Grampa's death, lies on a mattress hallucinating. A large woman enters the Joads' tent to pray for Granma's soul, but Ma sends the woman away, claiming that the old woman is too tired for such an ordeal.

Soon afterward, a policeman enters the tent and rudely informs Ma that the family will have to move on. When Tom returns to camp and reports that Noah has run off, Ma laments that the family is falling apart. The Joads must pack up and are forced to leave the Wilsons behind: Sairy's health is failing, and Ivy insists that the Joads move on without them. During the night, police stop the truck for a routine agricultural inspection. Ma pleads with the officer to let them go, saying that Granma is in desperate need of medical attention. When they cross into the valley, Ma reports that Granma has been dead since before the inspection. Ma lay with the body all night in the back of the truck.

ANALYSIS: CHAPTERS SIXTEEN–EIGHTEEN

The Joads' dreams about life in California stand in bold relief against the realities that they face. Rose of Sharon believes that Connie will study at night and make a life for her in town, but this fantasy rings rather hollow against the backdrop of Grampa's and now Granma's death. Coming after two sets of dire warnings from ruined migrant workers, Granma's death bodes especially ill for the Joads. They now seem fated to live out the cautionary tales of the men they have met in Chapters Sixteen and Eighteen, who now seem like a Greek chorus presaging impending tragedy. Before the Joads even set foot on its soil, California proves to be a land of vicious hostility rather than of opportunity. The cold manner of the police officers and border guards seems to testify to the harsh reception that awaits the family.

The sense of foreboding in this section is heightened as we witness the fulfillment of Ma Joad's greatest fear—the unraveling of the family. In addition to the grandparents' deaths, the reclusive Noah decides to remain alone on the river. Family is the foundation of the Joads' will to survive, for, as Chapter Seventeen makes clear, migrant families were able to endure the harsh circumstances of life on the road by uniting with other families. Collectively, they share a responsibility that would be too great for one family to bear alone. Moreover, whereas to share a burden is to lighten it, to share a dream is to intensify and concentrate it, making that dream more vivid. Thus "[t]he loss of home became one loss, and the golden time in the West was one dream." Interestingly, Steinbeck sandwiches these observations between two chapters in which the Joad family not only suffers a decrease in number but also meets with neighbors who have no interest in cooperating with them. Increasingly, then, these statements about the importance of togetherness serve not so much as an affirmation of the Joads' circumstances as an indication of what they are in the process of losing. The grandparents' deaths and Noah's departure are tragedies for the Joads.

Faced with these losses, Ma Joad demonstrates her strength as never before. Met by the deputy who evicts her from the camp and disdainfully calls her an "Okie," Ma chases the man away with a cast iron skillet. Similarly, she suffers privately with the knowledge of Granma's death so that the family can successfully cross the desert. These occurrences do take their toll on her: when Tom attempts to comfort her, she warns him not to touch her lest she fall apart. Still, her ability to endure adversity proves remarkable, as does her commitment to delivering her family, or as much of it as she can keep together, into a more prosperous life.

CHAPTERS NINETEEN–TWENTY-ONE

SUMMARY: CHAPTER NINETEEN

The narrator describes how California once belonged to Mexico but was taken away by hungry American squatters who believed that they owned the land because they farmed it. The descendants of these squatters are the wealthy farmers who defend their land with security guards and protect their wealth by paying their laborers extremely low wages. They resent the droves of "Okies" flooding into the state because they know that hungry and impoverished people are a danger to the stability of land ownership. For their part, the

Okies want only a decent wage and freedom from the threat of starvation. Settling in workers' camps, they try their best to look for work. Sometimes one of the them tries to grow a secret garden in a fallow field, but the deputies find it and destroy it.

SUMMARY: CHAPTER TWENTY

Because they do not have enough money for a proper burial, Ma and Pa Joad leave Granma's body in a coroner's office. They rejoin the family at Hooverville, a large, crowded, and dirty camp full of hungry families unable to find work. One young man, Floyd Knowles, tells Tom that when he encounters police, he must act "bull-simple": he must speak ramblingly and incoherently in order to convince the policeman that he is an unthreatening idiot. Floyd says that there are no jobs. Tom wonders why the men do not organize against the landowners, but Floyd says that anyone who discusses such possibilities will be labeled "red" and dragged off by the police. Men who attempt to organize are put on a "blacklist," which ensures that they will never find work. Casy discusses the injustice of the situation with Tom and wonders what he can do to help the suffering people. Connie tells Rose of Sharon that they should have stayed in Oklahoma, where he could have learned about tractors. She reminds him that he intends to study radios and that she "ain't gonna have this baby in no tent." Ma cooks a stew that attracts a bevy of hungry children. After feeding her family, she hands over the meager leftovers, which the children devour ravenously.

A contractor arrives in a new Chevrolet coupe to recruit workers for a fruit-picking job in Tulare County. When Knowles demands a contract and a set wage for the fruit pickers, the man summons a police deputy, who arrests Knowles on a bogus charge and then begins threatening the others. A scuffle ensues. Knowles runs off, and the deputy shoots at him recklessly, piercing a woman through the hand. Tom trips the deputy, and Casy, coming from behind, knocks him unconscious. Knowing that someone will need to be held accountable, Casy volunteers, reminding Tom that he has broken parole by leaving Oklahoma. Backup officers arrive and arrest Casy. The sheriff announces that the whole camp will now be burned.

Uncle John is distraught by Casy's sacrifice. Uncle John had spoken with Casy about the nature of sin, and now that the former preacher is gone, John's wife's tragic death lies heavy upon him. He tells the family that he must get drunk or he will not be able to bear his sorrow. They allow him to go buy alcohol. Rose of Sharon asks if anyone has seen Connie, and Al says that he saw him walking south along the river. Pa insists that Connie was always a good-for-nothing, but Rose of Sharon is beside herself with grief at his absence. Meanwhile, convinced that his family needs to leave the camp before further trouble erupts, Tom rounds up Uncle John, knocking the man unconscious in order to get him on the truck. The Joads depart, leaving word at the camp store for Connie in case he returns. Coming upon a nearby town, the family is turned away by a crowd of pick-handle and shotgun wielding men, who have stationed themselves by the road to keep Okies out. Tom is enraged, but Ma Joad reminds him that a "different time's comin'."

SUMMARY: CHAPTER TWENTY-ONE
The hostility directed toward the migrants changes them and brings them together. Property owners are terrified of "the flare of want in the eyes of the migrants." California locals form armed bands to terrorize the "Okies" and keep them in their place. The owners of large farms drive the smaller farmers out of business, making more and more people destitute and unable to feed themselves or their children.

ANALYSIS: CHAPTERS NINETEEN–TWENTY-ONE
Chapters Nineteen and Twenty-One act like a refrain in their repetition of the novel's social criticism. Both present history—especially California's history—as a battle between the rich and the poor. Founded by squatters who stole the land from Mexicans, California has been the setting for a series of desperate measures taken by "frantic hungry men." The landowners fear that history will repeat itself, and that the migrant farmers, who crave land and sustenance, will take their livelihood from them. The migrants, however, seeing acre upon acre of unused land, dream of tending just enough of it to support their families. The migrants' simple desire to produce, and the landowners' resistance, receives particularly poignant illustration in the tale of the man who plants a few carrots and turnips in a fallow field.

Chapter Twenty finds the Joads in Hooverville, where harsh reality further intrudes upon their idealistic vision of solidarity. The Joads have already encountered fellow migrants who do not share their desire to cooperate. The men who have failed to make a living in California, for example, show little interest in joining forces with the family. Disillusioned by their experiences, these men openly doubt and even mock the Joads' optimism. This unfriendliness, combined with an intensifying scarcity of resources, makes it increasingly difficult for the Joads to honor bonds other than those of kinship. The scene in which Ma Joad prepares her stew offers a powerful illustration of this. Here, the scarcity of food forces her to walk a thin line between selfish interest in her own family and generosity toward the larger community. Yet, while Ma looks to the needs of her family first, she does manage to do what she can to alleviate some of the hunger of the onlooking children. Her compassion toward these strangers, whom she nonetheless considers her people, elevates her above the bleak and hateful circumstances that surround her.

While Ma expresses her devotion to community by sharing her stew with her fellow migrants' children, Tom and Casy begin to express this devotion in more overtly political ways and with a sense of often violent outrage. The incident surrounding Floyd Knowles and the fruit-picking contractor signifies the beginning of the two men's involvement in the burgeoning movement to organize migrant labor, to protect workers against unfair treatment and unlivable wages. Although the men have always possessed a sense for injustice, they do not act on their convictions until they witness Floyd Knowles's impassioned speech against unfair labor practices. While the hardships facing the family serve to kindle devotions in some, they serve to rupture loyalties in others. Connie's decision to abandon his wife and unborn child affects Rose of Sharon deeply and constitutes a turning point for her. His departure disabuses the girl of all notions of a charmed life in the big city and forces her to come to terms with the conditions in which she lives.

CHAPTERS TWENTY-TWO–TWENTY-FOUR

SUMMARY: CHAPTER TWENTY-TWO

> [T]hat police. He done somepin to me, made me feel
> mean . . . ashamed. An' now I ain't ashamed . . . Why, I
> feel like people again.
>
> (See QUOTATIONS, p. 44)

Later that night, the Joads come across the Weedpatch camp, a decent, government-sponsored facility where migrants govern themselves, thus avoiding the abuse of corrupt police officers. Appointed committees ensure that the grounds remain clean and equipped with working toilets and showers. Early in the morning after their arrival, Tom wakes and meets Timothy and Wilkie Wallace, who invite him to breakfast. They agree to take him to the ranch they have been working on to see if they can get him a job. At the ranch, the boss, Mr. Thomas, tells the men about the Farmers' Association, which demands that he pay his laborers twenty-five cents an hour and no more. Even though he knows his men deserve a higher wage, Thomas claims that to pay more would "only cause unrest." He goes on to say that the government camp makes the association extremely uncomfortable: the members believe the place to be riddled with communists, or "red agitators." In hopes of shutting the facilities down, Mr. Thomas says, the association is planning to send instigators into the camp on Saturday night to start a riot. The police will then have the right to enter the camp, arrest the labor organizers, and evict the migrants.

Back at the camp, the rest of the Joad men go to find work, and Ma is visited by Jim Rawley, the camp manager, whose kindness makes her feel human again. A religious fanatic named Mrs. Sandry appears and tells Rose of Sharon to beware of the dancing and sinning that goes on in the camp: the babies of sinners, she warns, are born "dead and bloody." The camp's Ladies Committee then drops in on Ma and Rose of Sharon, introducing the women to the rules of the camp. Pa, Al, and Uncle John return from a day of fruitless searching for work, but Ma remains hopeful, for Tom has been hired.

SUMMARY: CHAPTER TWENTY-THREE
When the people are not working or looking for work, they make music and tell folktales together. If they have money, they can buy alcohol, which, like music, temporarily distracts them from their miseries. Preachers give fire-and-brimstone sermons about evil and sin, haranguing the people until they grovel on the ground, and conduct mass baptisms. These are the various methods the migrants have for finding escape and salvation.

SUMMARY: CHAPTER TWENTY-FOUR
It is the night of the camp dance—the night that the Farmers' Association plans to start a riot and have the camp shut down. Ezra Huston, the chairman of the camp committee, hires twenty men to look out for instigators and preempt the riot. Although Rose of Sharon goes to the event, she decides not to dance for fear of the effect it might have on her baby. As the music begins, Tom and the other men

quickly spot three dubious-looking men. They watch the men carefully. When one of the suspected troublemakers picks a fight by stepping in to dance with another man's date, the men apprehend the trio and evict them from the camp. Before they leave, Huston asks the three why they would turn against their own brethren, and the men confess that they have been well paid to start a riot. Later that night, a man tells a story about a group of mountain people who were hired as cheap labor by a rubber company in Akron. When the mountain people joined a union, the townspeople united to run them out of town. In response, five thousand mountain men marched through the center of town with their rifles, allegedly to shoot turkeys on the far side of the settlement. The march served as a powerful demonstration. The storyteller concludes that there has been no trouble between the townspeople and the workers since then.

ANALYSIS: CHAPTERS TWENTY-TWO–TWENTY-FOUR

Life in the Weedpatch government camp proves to turn the Joads' luck around. Perhaps for the first time since leaving Oklahoma, the family finds itself in a secure position. Tom finds a job, and the camp manager treats Ma with such dignity that she says she feels "like people again." The charity, kindness, and goodwill that the migrants exhibit toward one another testifies to the power of their fellowship. When left to their own devices, and given shelter from the corrupt social system that keeps them down, the migrants make the first steps toward establishing an almost utopian mini-society. Moreover, life in Weedpatch disproves the landowners' beliefs that "Okies" lead undignified, uncivilized lives. Indeed, the migrants show themselves to be more civilized than the landowners, as demonstrated by the way in which they respond to the Farmers' Association's plot to sabotage the camp. Most of the wealthy landowners believe that poverty-stricken, uneducated farmers deserve to be treated contemptuously. These men maintain that to reward farmers with amenities such as toilets, showers, and comfortable wages will merely give them a sense of entitlement, embolden them to ask for more, and thus create social and economic unrest. The migrants, however, meet the association's scheming and violent plot with grace and integrity. Here, the farmers rise far above the men who oppress them by exhibiting a kind of dignity that, in the world Steinbeck describes, often eludes the rich.

The Joads' experiences in the Weedpatch camp serve to illustrate one of the novel's main theses: humans find their greatest strength in numbers. When Ma tries to help Rose of Sharon to overcome her grief at Connie's abandonment, she reminds the girl, "[Y]ou're jest one person, an' they's a lot of other folks." As the novel has suggested time and again, the needs of the group supersede the needs of the individual. As the novel moves into its final chapters, this philosophy takes center stage. The unity of the migrants poses the greatest threat to landowners and the socioeconomic system on which they thrive. This idea begins to dawn on the farmers, who realize the effects that their numbers, once organized, might have. The story about the rubber workers and their mass march indicates the desperation of people in these times to obtain not only economic solvency but the respect they deserve as human beings.

As Tom's political involvement increases, the reader notes a change in his character. At the beginning of the novel, Tom asserted that he was interested only in getting through the present day; thinking about the future proved too troubling a task. Now, however, devoted as he is to his family and his fellow migrants, Tom begins to look toward the future and its possibilities.

The Weedpatch camp changes not only individual characters but also the interactions among groups of characters. Thus, we witness a shift of power taking place within the Joad clan. Always a source of strength and indomitable love, Ma Joad begins to move into a space traditionally reserved for male family members: as Pa Joad suffers one failure after another, Ma is called upon to make decisions and guide the family. The altered family structure parallels the more general revision of traditional power structures in the camp. The farmers now make their own decisions, delegating duties according to notions of fairness and common sense rather than adhering to old hierarchies or submitting to individual cravings for control. As Jim Casy had predicted in Chapter Ten when he insisted on helping Ma salt the family's meat, when faced with unprecedented hardship, people can no longer afford to stratify themselves according to gender, age, or other superficial differences.

Chapters Twenty-Five–Twenty-Seven

Summary: Chapter Twenty-Five

Spring is beautiful in California, but, like the migrants, many small local farmers stand to be ruined by large landowners, who monopolize the industry. Unable to compete with these magnates, small farmers watch their crops wither and their debts rise. The wine in the vineyards' vats goes bad, and anger and resentment spread throughout the land. The narrator comments, "In the souls of the people, the grapes of wrath are filling and growing heavy, growing heavy for the vintage."

SUMMARY: CHAPTER TWENTY-SIX

After nearly a month in the government camp, the Joads find their supplies running low and work scarce. Ma Joad convinces the others that they must leave the camp the next day. They make preparations and say good-bye to their friends. The truck has a flat tire, and as they are fixing it, a man in a suit and heavy jewelry pulls up in a roadster with news of employment: the Joads can go to work picking peaches only thirty-five miles away. When they arrive at the peach farm, they find cars backed up on the roads leading to it, and angry mobs of people shout from the roadside. The family learns that they will be paid only five cents a box for picking peaches; desperate for food, they take the job. At the end of the day, even with everyone in the family working, they have earned only one dollar. They must spend their entire day's wages on their meal that night, and afterward they remain hungry.

That evening, Al goes looking for girls, and Tom, curious about the trouble on the roadside, goes to investigate. Guards turn him away at the orchard gate, but Tom sneaks under the gate and starts down the road. He comes upon a tent and discovers that one of the men inside is Jim Casy. Jim tells him about his experience in prison and reports that he now works to organize the migrant farmers. He explains that the owner of the peach orchards cut wages to two-and-a-half cents a box, so the men went on strike. Now the owner has hired a new group of men in hopes of breaking the strike. Casy predicts that by tomorrow, even the strike-breakers will be making only two-and-a-half cents per box. Tom and Casy see flashlight beams, and two policemen approach them, recognizing Casy as the workers' leader and referring to him as a communist. As Casy protests that the men are only helping to starve children, one of them crushes his skull with a pick handle. Tom flies into a rage and wields the pick handle on Casy's murderer, killing him before receiving a blow to his own head. He manages to run away and makes it back to his family. In the morning, when they discover his wounds and hear his story, Tom offers to leave so as not to bring any trouble to them. Ma, however, insists that he stay. They leave the peach farm and head off to find work picking cotton. Tom hides in a culvert close to the plantation—his crushed nose and bruised face would bring suspicion upon him—and the family sneaks food to him.

SUMMARY: CHAPTER TWENTY-SEVEN
Signs appear everywhere advertising work in the cotton fields. Wages are decent, but workers without cotton-picking sacks are forced to buy them on credit. There are so many workers that some are unable to do enough work even to pay for their sacks. Some of the owners are crooked and rig the scales used to weigh the cotton. To counter this practice, the migrants often load stones in their sacks.

ANALYSIS: CHAPTERS TWETNY-FIVE–TWENTY-SEVEN
In the short, expository chapters that intersperse the story of the Joads, Steinbeck employs a range of prose styles and tones. He ranges from overt symbolism (as with the turtle in Chapter Three), to heated sermonizing (as with his indictment of corrupt businessmen in Chapter Seven), to the didactic tone of a parable (as with the story of Mae the waitress in Chapter Fifteen). In this part of the book, Steinbeck turns to the rough, native language of the people to convey a day on a cotton farm (Chapter Twenty-Seven): the effect is an intimate, lively, and moving portrayal of the daily life of the migrants. In Chapter Twenty-Five, the phrasing and word choice evokes biblical language: simple and declarative, yet highly stylized and symbolic. Steinbeck portrays the rotten state of the economic system by describing the literal decay that results from this system's agricultural mismanagement. Depictions of the putrefying crops symbolize the people's darkening, festering anger. The rotting vines and spoiled vintage in particular, both a source and an emblem of the workers' rage, become a central image and provide the novel with its title.

The Joads' dream of a golden life in California, like the season's wine, has gone sour. After a month in the government camp with little work, the family's resources are dangerously low. The few days of charmed living have passed. Desperate and discouraged, Ma announces that the family needs to move on; her seizure of authority rocks the traditional family structure. Pa is upset that Ma has assumed the task of decision-making, a responsibility that typically belongs to the male head of the household. When he threatens to put her back in her "proper place," Ma responds by saying, "[Y]ou ain't a-doin' your job. . . . If you was, why, you could use your stick, an' women folks'd sniffle their nose and creep-mouse aroun'. " The family structure has undergone a revolution, in which the female figure, traditionally powerless, has taken control, while the male figure, traditionally in the leadership role, has retreated.

In this section, the stakes of the conflict established in previous chapters are made clear: the contest between rich and poor, between landowners and migrants, is one that will—and perhaps must—be fought to the death. As the end of Chapter Twenty-Five states, the people's anger is ripening, "growing heavy for the vintage." In other words, their anger must soon be released in a burst of violence. When that happens, lives will be lost. Casy's death stands as a sober reminder of the price that must be paid for equality.

CHAPTERS TWENTY-EIGHT–THIRTY

SUMMARY: CHAPTER TWENTY-EIGHT

> *Wherever they's a fight so hungry people can eat, I'll be there.... An' when our folks eat [what] they raise an' live in the houses they build ... I'll be there.*
> *(See* QUOTATIONS, *p. 46)*

SUMMARY & ANALYSIS

At the cotton fields, the Joads are given a boxcar to live in, but they are forced to share it with another family, the Wainwrights. They soon make enough money to buy food and clothing, and Ma Joad is even able to indulge and treat Ruthie and Winfield to a box of Cracker Jack candy. When another girl, envious of Ruthie's treat, picks a fight with her, Ruthie boasts angrily that her older brother has killed two men and is now in hiding. Ma Joad hurries into the woods to warn Tom that his secret has been revealed. Sorrowfully, she urges him to leave lest he be caught. Tom shares with his mother some of Jim Casy's words of wisdom, which he has been pondering since his friend died: every man's soul is simply a small piece of a great soul. Tom says that he has decided to unify his soul with this great soul by working to organize the people, as Casy would have wanted. Ma reminds Tom that Casy died for his efforts, but Tom jokes that he will be faster to duck out of harm's way. As Ma returns to the boxcar, the owner of a small farm stops her and tells her he needs pickers for his twenty acres. Ma brings the news of the job back to the boxcar, where Al announces that he and Agnes Wainwright plan to be married. The families celebrate.

The next day, the two families travel to the small plantation, where so many workers have amassed that the entire crop is picked before noon. Glumly, the family returns to the boxcar, and it begins to rain.

SUMMARY: CHAPTER TWENTY-NINE

Rain lashes the land, and no work can be done during the deluge. Rivers overflow, and cars wash away in the coursing mud. The men are forced to beg and to steal food. The women watch the men in apprehension, worried that they might finally see them break. Instead, however, they see the men's fear turning to anger. The women know that their men will remain strong as long as they can maintain their rage.

SUMMARY: CHAPTER THIRTY

The rain continues to fall. On the third day of the storm, the skies still show no sign of clearing. Rose of Sharon, sick and feverish, goes into labor. The truck has flooded, and the family has no choice but to remain in the boxcar. At Pa's urging, the men work to build a makeshift dam to keep the water from flooding their shelter or washing it away. However, an uprooted tree cascades into the dam and destroys it. When Pa Joad enters the car, soaked and defeated, Mrs. Wainwright informs him that Rose of Sharon has delivered a stillborn baby. The family sends Uncle John to bury the child. He ventures into the storm, places the improvised coffin in the stream, and watches the current carry it away. The rains continue. Pa spends the last of the family's money on food.

On the sixth day of rain, the flood begins to overtake the boxcar, and Ma decides that the family must seek dry ground. Al decides to stay with the Wainwrights and Agnes. Traveling on foot, the remaining Joads spot a barn and head toward it. There, they find a dying man and small boy. The boy tells them that his father has not eaten for six days, having given all available food to his son. The man's health has deteriorated to such an extent that he cannot digest solid food; he needs soup or milk. Ma looks to Rose of Sharon, and the girl at once understands her unstated thoughts. Rose of Sharon asks everyone to leave the barn and, once alone, she approaches the starving man. Despite his protests, she holds him close and suckles him.

ANALYSIS: CHAPTERS TWENTY-EIGHT–THIRTY

The end of *The Grapes of Wrath* is among the most memorable concluding chapters in American literature. Tom continues the legacy of Jim Casy as he promises to live his life devoted to a soul greater than his own. Recognizing the truth in the teachings of the Christ-like Casy, Tom realizes that a person's highest calling is to put him- or herself in the service of the collective good. As Tom leaves his family to fight for social justice, he completes the transformation that began several chapters earlier. Initially lacking the patience and energy to consider the future at all, he marches off to lead the struggle toward making that future a kinder and gentler one.

Without Tom, and without food or work, the Joads sink, in the novel's final chapter, to their most destitute moment yet. Nonetheless, the book ends on a surprisingly hopeful note: Steinbeck uses a collection of symbols, most of them borrowed from biblical stories, to inject a deeply spiritual optimism into his bleak tale. Thus, while the rain represents a damaging force that threatens to wash away the few possessions the Joads have left, it also represents a power of renewal. The reader recalls Steinbeck's phrasing in Chapter Twenty-Nine, in which the text notes that the downpours, although causing great destruction, also enable the coming of spring: we read that the raindrops are followed by "[t]iny points of grass," making the hills a pale green.

Even the events surrounding the birth of the dead baby contain images of hope. As Uncle John floats the child downstream, Steinbeck invokes the story of Moses, who, as a baby, was sent down the Nile, and later delivered his people out of slavery and into the Promised Land of Israel. As John surrenders the tiny body to the currents, he tells it: "Go down an' tell 'em. Go down in the street an' rot an' tell 'em that way. That's the way you can talk." The child's corpse becomes a symbolic messenger, charged with the task of testifying to his people's suffering. (Again, in John's speech we find an allusion to the life of the Hebrew prophet: his words echo the refrain of the traditional folk gospel song "Go Down, Moses.")

> *Says . . . he jus' got a little piece of a great big soul. Says . . . [his piece] wasn't no good 'less it was with the rest, an' was whole.*
>
> (See QUOTATIONS, p. 45)

The closing image of the novel is imbued with equal spiritual power as Rose of Sharon and the starving man in the barn form the figure of a Pietà—a famous motif in visual art in which the Virgin Mary holds the dead Christ in her lap. As Rose of Sharon suckles the dying man, we watch her transform from the complaining, naive, often self-centered girl of previous chapters into a figure of maternal love. As a mother whose child has been sacrificed to send a larger message to the world, she assumes a role similar to that of the mother of Christ. Like Mary, she represents ultimate comfort and protection from suffering, confirming an image of the world in which generosity and self-sacrifice are the greatest of virtues.

Important Quotations Explained

1. I got thinkin' how we was holy when we was one thing, an'
    mankin' was holy when it was one thing. An' it on'y got
    unholy when one mis'able little fella got the bit in his teeth
    an' run off his own way, kickin' an' draggin' an' fightin'.
    Fella like that bust the holi-ness. But when they're all
    workin' together, not one fella for another fella, but one fella
    kind of harnessed to the whole shebang—that's right, that's
    holy.

In Chapter Eight, after Tom and Jim Casy arrive at Uncle John's
farm, the family convinces the ex-preacher to say grace over their
breakfast. Casy hesitates, but eventually offers these words. They
constitute, in short, the philosophy that governs the novel: both
Casy and, later, Tom will put this theory into practice by way of a
revolutionary fight for the rights of their fellow man—their efforts
to organize the migrant workers. In the end, Casy proves willing to
lose his life in this struggle, and Tom, picking up where his mentor
left off, resolves to unify his soul with the greater soul of human-
kind.

    On a smaller scale, the Joad family also lives up to this philoso-
phy, determinedly cooperating with fellow migrant workers and
offering them their services or their food. Ma Joad in particular
emphasizes the importance of keeping the family together. She
believes deeply in the power of human bonds to provide not only
practical benefits but spiritual sustenance.

2. The last clear definite function of man—muscles aching to
    work, minds aching to create beyond the single need—this is
    man. To build a wall, to build a house, a dam, and in the wall
    and house and dam to put something of Manself, and to
    Manself take back something of the wall, the house the dam;
    to take hard muscles from the lifting, to take the clear lines
    and form from conceiving. For man, unlike any other thing
    organic or inorganic in the universe, grows beyond his

work, walks up the stairs of his concepts, emerges ahead of his accomplishments.

These lines exemplify the exalted and highly stylized tone found in the brief expository chapters that punctuate the story of the Joads. Linguistically, the passage adopts an almost biblical tenor in its repetition and grandeur: "To build a wall, to build a house, a dam, and in the wall and house and dam to put something of Manself." The quotation also exhibits a moral simplicity evocative of biblical parable: man toils, and his labor builds him as a person.

In his emphasis on the spiritual necessity of work, Steinbeck makes a point that is crucial to his overarching message in the book: while the workers' rights movement demands higher wages and fairer treatment, it does not demand an alleviation of hard work per se. Rather, the movement seeks to restore the dignity of hard work to the migrants. When the workers are respected, when expectations are high and achievement acknowledged, this is when human beings can begin to find in their labor the transcendence here described.

3. "We're Joads. We don't look up to nobody. Grampa's grampa, he fit in the Revolution. We was farm people till the debt. And then—them people. They done somepin to us. Ever' time they come seemed like they was a-whippin' me— all of us. An' in Needles, that police. He done somepin to me, made me feel mean. Made me feel ashamed. An' now I ain't ashamed. These folks is our folks—is our folks. An' that manager, he come an' set an' drank coffee, an' he says, 'Mrs. Joad' this, an' 'Mrs. Joad' that—an' 'How you gettin' on, Mrs. Joad?'" She stopped and sighed. "Why, I feel like people again."

After the Joads arrive in the Weedpatch government camp in Chapter Twenty-Two, Ma discusses the effects of life on the road. It has, she reports, changed her. The open gestures of hostility the family has suffered at the hands of policemen and landowners have made her "mean," petty, hardened. In Weedpatch, however, for the first time since leaving Oklahoma she is treated like a human being. The camp manager's kindness rekindles her sense of connection in the world: "These is our folks," she says. Ma's speech underlines the importance of fellowship among the migrants, suggesting that, given their current difficulties, one cannot afford to bear one's burdens alone.

Throughout *The Grapes of Wrath,* Steinbeck emphasizes the importance of the self-respect and sense of dignity that Ma displays here. The unfair treatment the migrants receive does not simply create hardship for them; it diminishes them as human beings. As long as people maintain a sense of injustice, however—a sense of anger against those who seek to undercut their pride in themselves—they will never lose their dignity. This notion is reinforced particularly at the end of the book, in the images of the festering grapes of wrath (Chapter Twenty-Five) and in the last of the short, expository chapters (Chapter Twenty-Nine), in which the worker women, watching their husbands and brothers and sons, know that these men will remain strong "as long as fear [can] turn to wrath."

4.   Says one time he went out in the wilderness to find his own
      soul, an' he foun' he didn't have no soul that was his'n. Says
      he foun' he jus' got a little piece of a great big soul. Says a
      wilderness ain't no good, 'cause his little piece of a soul
      wasn't no good 'less it was with the rest, an' was whole.

As Tom bids good-bye to Ma Joad in Chapter Twenty-Eight, he relates to her this bit of Jim Casy's wisdom. His statement not only echoes Casy's definition of holiness in Chapter Eight but also testifies to the transformation of Tom's character. Enlightened by his friend's teaching and his own experiences, Tom no longer focuses his energies only on the present moment. Instead, realizing his responsibility to his fellow human beings, he starts on a path toward bettering the future, helping generations of workers yet to come. In this way, Tom becomes more than just "a little piece of a great big soul"; he joins with a universal spirit, thereby becoming "whole."

The quotation also speaks to Casy's notion, questioned at times in the rest of the novel, that a human-to-human connection always takes precedence over an individual's connection to the land. Casy has acknowledged the spiritual value of nature by going out into "the wilderness" to find his soul, but he has found that the wilderness offers no sustenance for his spirit unless he feels joined to other human spirits. Other characters in the novel seem to contest this view: Grampa refuses to leave the Oklahoma farm and must be drugged so that the family can load him into the truck; the Joads' neighbor, Muley Graves, similarly refused to leave for California

QUOTATIONS

with his family, and ultimately succeeded in sending them on without him. Both men represent an understandable reluctance to be separated from their land: the land has shaped their identities and constitutes part of who they are. But the Joads, like Casy, believe ultimately in the superior ability of interpersonal connections to sustain their grandfather's life and spirit. Although Grampa dies soon after the trip begins, he has not died a lonely death.

5. Wherever they's a fight so hungry people can eat, I'll be there. Wherever they's a cop beatin' up a guy, I'll be there. If Casy knowed, why, I'll be in the way guys yell when they're mad an'—I'll be in the way kids laugh when they're hungry n' they know supper's ready. An' when our folks eat the stuff they raise an' live in the houses they build—why, I'll be there. See? God, I'm talkin' like Casy. Comes of thinkin' about him so much. Seems like I can see him sometimes.

The death of Jim Casy completes the transformation of Tom Joad into a man ready to take responsibility for the future and to act accordingly. Throughout the novel, Casy acts as Steinbeck's moral mouthpiece, articulating several of the book's more important themes, such as the sanctity of human life and the necessary unity of all mankind. In this passage, from Chapter Twenty-Eight, Tom quiets Ma's fear that he, like Casy, will lose his life in the workers' movement. Tom assures her that regardless of whether he lives or dies, his spirit will continue on in the triumphs and turmoil of the world. As the Joads are torn apart, Tom's words offer the promise of a deep, lasting connection that no tragedy can break.

QUOTATIONS

KEY FACTS

FULL TITLE
The Grapes of Wrath

AUTHOR
John Steinbeck

TYPE OF WORK
Novel

GENRE
Epic; realistic fiction; social commentary

LANGUAGE
English

TIME AND PLACE WRITTEN
Late May–late October 1938, Los Gatos, CA

DATE OF FIRST PUBLICATION
April 14, 1939

PUBLISHER
The Viking Press

NARRATOR
An anonymous, all-knowing, historically aware consciousness that is deeply sympathetic, not only to the migrants but to workers, the poor, and the dispossessed generally.

POINT OF VIEW
The narrative shifts dramatically between different points of view. In some chapters the narrator describes events broadly, summarizing the experiences of a large number of people and providing historical analysis. Frequently, in the same chapters, the narrator assumes the voice of a typical individual, such as a displaced farmer or a crooked used-car salesman, expressing that person's individual concerns. When the narrator assumes the voice of an anonymous individual, the words sometimes sound like what an actual person might say, but sometimes they form a highly poetic representation of the anonymous indiv-idual's thoughts and soul. The chapters focusing on the Joad family are

narrated primarily from an objective point of view, representing conversations and interactions without focusing on any particular character. Here, the characters' actions are presented as an observer might witness them, without directly representing the characters' thoughts and motivations. At certain points, however, the narrator shifts and presents the Joads from an omniscient point of view, explaining their psychologies, characters, and motivations in intimate detail.

TONE
Mournful, awed, enraged, sympathetic

TENSE
Mainly past

SETTING (TIME)
Late 1930s

SETTING (PLACE)
Oklahoma, California, and points along the way

PROTAGONIST
Tom Joad

MAJOR CONFLICT
The disastrous drought of the 1930s forces farmers to migrate westward to California, pitting migrants against locals and property owners against the destitute. Moreover, Tom Joad's story dramatizes a conflict between the impulse to respond to hardship and disaster by focusing on one's own needs and the impulse to risk one's safety by working for a common good.

RISING ACTION
Tom is released from prison, determined to mind his own business; Tom encounters the devastation of the Dust Bowl; Casy presents Tom with his philosophy of the holiness of human beings in general; Tom is drawn into the workers' movement.

CLIMAX
A policeman murders Casy and Tom kills the policeman, making himself an outlaw and committing himself totally to the cause of workers' rights rather than the fortunes of his own family.

KEY FACTS

FALLING ACTION

Tom's explanation to Ma of the wisdom he learned from Casy;
Tom's departure from the rest of the Joad family; Rose of
Sharon's nursing of the starving man, which symbolizes the
community in suffering formed by the destitute migrants.

THEMES

Man's inhumanity to man; the saving power of family and
fellowship; the dignity of wrath; the multiplying effects of
altruism and selfishness

MOTIFS

Improvised leadership structures

SYMBOLS

Rose of Sharon's pregnancy; the death of the Joads' dog

FORESHADOWING

Many tragedies or reported tragedies in the book serve to
foreshadow future sorrows. Thus, the death of the grandparents
and the reports of men returning in despair from California are
sources of sadness in themselves, but they also seem to bode ill
for the future. Moreover, the descriptive chapters that are
interspersed with the book's Joad-focused chapters often serve to
foreshadow tragedy: at many points, they portray hardships
facing the migrants at large, which the Joads then encounter in
the following chapter.

KEY FACTS

Study Questions & Essay Topics

Study Questions

1. *Half of the chapters in The Grapes of Wrath focus on the dramatic westward journey of the Joad family, while the others possess a broader scope, providing a more general picture of the migration of thousands of Dust Bowl farmers. Discuss this structure. Why might Steinbeck have chosen it? How do the two kinds of chapters reinforce each other?*

The Grapes of Wrath is most memorable as the story of the Joad family's trek across Depression-era America. The long narrative chapters that trace their journey provide a personal context for understanding the more abstract social, historical, and symbolic musings of the shorter alternating chapters. Despite their sometimes preachy tone, these alternating chapters play an important role in the structure of the novel. Most notably, they extend the saga of migrant farmers beyond a single family, reminding the reader that the hardships faced by the Joads were widespread, afflicting tens of thousands of families in the Dust Bowl. Furthermore, these chapters anticipate the circumstances that the Joads will encounter: when the Joads come to Hooverville in Chapter Twenty, for instance, the reader has already read a detailed description of these camps in the preceding chapter and thus foresees their difficulties.

Alternating between the Joads' tale and more contextual musings outside the narrative also allows Steinbeck to employ a greater range of writing styles. It is true that Steinbeck successfully conveys a great deal of the Joads' journey through spare, declarative prose and through the rustic dialect of the family members. However, the short chapters allow him to exceed the constraints of these prose forms, to root his story in a more universal tradition. At times, Steinbeck evokes the repetition and moral bluntness of biblical tales; at other moments, he assumes the clear, castigating tone of a soapbox politician; sometimes his style conjures up ancient epics of heroic deeds and archetypal struggles. Thus, the author roots his story in a more universal tradition, endowing it with significance that exceeds the individual characters and their specific setting.

2. *What is Jim Casy's role in the novel? How does his moral philosophy govern the novel as a whole?*

Jim Casy is, in many ways, the novel's guiding moral voice. He explicitly articulates many of Steinbeck's thematic ideas, namely that human life is as sacred as any divinity and that a single life has little purpose unless it takes part in, and contributes to, a greater community. These ideas provide the foundation for the acts of charity and kindness that unify the migrant farmers as their lives grow harder and less forgiving.

Furthermore, Casy plays a vital role in the transformation of Tom Joad into a social activist. In many ways, Casy resembles a Christ figure: he is a man possessed of radical, controversial ideas; a champion of the poor and oppressed; and, in the end, a martyr for his beliefs. Tom's newfound commitment to a better future indicates that Casy was correct in positing the power of selfless devotion to others: by joining the cause to help the people, and by inspiring others to join as well, Casy ensures his own immortality. Because he has merged his spirit with the whole of humanity, Casy lives on.

3. *Many critics have noted the sense of gritty, unflinching realism pervading The Grapes of Wrath. How does Steinbeck achieve this effect? Do his character portrayals contribute, or his description of setting, or both?*

The book's sense of realism results from its brutal setting. The migrants exist in a world characterized by dirt, dust, suffering, starvation, death, poverty, ignorance, prejudice, and despair. Steinbeck does not hesitate to provide honest details, many of which appear in the brief chapters of exposition and social commentary that intersperse the Joads' story.

In contrast to the naturalistic setting, many of the characters in the Joad family stand as sentimentalized or heroicized figures. The realism of the nonnarrative chapters, some of which function like journalistic or cinematic reportage, balances this more romantic side of the novel by grounding the reader in the undeniably harsh

QUESTIONS & ESSAYS

and vivid surroundings. While Steinbeck's frequent romanticism contributes to his novel's epic proportion and import, his use of realism strengthens the novel's effectiveness as a work of social commentary.

SUGGESTED ESSAY TOPICS

1. *Discuss the development of Tom Joad as a character. How does he grow throughout the book? What effects do Jim Casy's imprisonment and death have on his development?*

2. *Discuss the ending of the novel. Does it fit aesthetically with the rest of the book? Is it believable for Rose of Sharon to assume the role of a transcendent giver of life? Does the ending effectively embody thematic trends within the novel's development? Does it provide hope, or does it leave the reader unsettled?*

3. *The third chapter of the novel depicts a turtle crossing the Oklahoma highway. How does this chapter symbolize the story of the migrants?*

4. *Think about the book in terms of Steinbeck's intent for it. Do you think it successfully raises sympathy for the plight of the Dust Bowl farmers, or does it seem untrustworthy in some way?*

REVIEW & RESOURCES

QUIZ

1. How does Grampa die?

    A. He has a stroke
    B. He has a heart attack
    C. He dies of old age
    D. Noah kills him

2. Why is Noah slightly deformed?

    A. Ma drank heavily during her pregnancy
    B. A local corporation dumped pollutants into the water supply
    C. Pa tried to deliver Noah by pulling him out with his bare hands
    D. As a child, Noah was run over by a combine

3. What is a "big cat"?

    A. A machine used by the banks to evict farmers
    B. The migrants' nickname for a policeman
    C. The policemen's nickname for a male Okie
    D. A terrible dust storm

4. During what decade did the Dust Bowl tragedy take place?

    A. The 1910s
    B. The 1920s
    C. The 1930s
    D. The 1940s

5. How many years was Tom in prison?

    A. 11
    B. 14
    C. 2
    D. 4

6. What does Uncle John give to children?

    A. Pennies
    B. Cracker Jack
    C. Gum
    D. Wooden soldiers

7. According to Chapter Nineteen, who were the first Americans to settle California?

    A. Squatters
    B. Middle-class businesspeople
    C. Gold diggers
    D. Cowboys

8. Who is given the task of burying Rose of Sharon's stillborn child?

    A. Uncle John
    B. Tom
    C. Pa Joad
    D. Agnes Wainwright

9. What are Al's main interests?

    A. Cars and clothes
    B. Music and girls
    C. Girls and cars
    D. Music and clothes

10. Where do the Joads leave Granma's corpse?

    A. A coroner's office
    B. A hospital morgue
    C. Under a sycamore tree
    D. By the banks of a stream

11. Which Joad child believes him- or herself to be the least loved by Ma and Pa?

    A. Rose of Sharon
    B. Tom
    C. Al
    D. Noah

12. What was Jim Casy's former occupation?

    A. Truck driver
    B. Preacher
    C. Ditch digger
    D. Mayor

13. How does Jim Casy die?

    A. He dies of heat exhaustion in the fields
    B. He kills himself out of sheer despair
    C. He dies of starvation
    D. He dies in a fight during a workers' strike

14. What do the citizens of California angrily call the migrants?

    A Hobos
    B. Okies
    C. Riffraff
    D. Bonzos

15. At the end of the novel, who is the leader of the Joad family?

    A. Pa Joad
    B. Tom Joad
    C. Grampa Joad
    D. Ma Joad

16. Whom does Agnes Wainwright decide to marry?

    A. Tom
    B. Al
    C. Jim Casy
    D. Floyd Knowles

17. Who in the novel first proposes the idea of organizing the workers?

    A. Tom
    B. Al
    C. Jim Casy
    D. Floyd Knowles

18. Why does Pa's dam fail?

 A. Pa uses sand when he should have used mortar
 B. A tree falls into it
 C. The water simply rises too fast
 D. Pa builds a good dam, but he builds it in a bad place

19. Why does Ruthie reveal Tom's secret?

 A. She is jealous of her older brother
 B. She talks in her sleep
 C. She wants to frighten a policeman
 D. She wants to impress a girl who is picking on her

20. Who tells Tom his parents' whereabouts when he arrives at their deserted farm?

 A. Jim
 B. Muley Graves
 C. Winifred
 D. Mr. Huston

21. In what year did *The Grapes of Wrath* win a Pulitzer Prize?

 A. 1940
 B. 1936
 C. 1939
 D. 1962

22. Why does Ma fear that Winfield will grow up to be wild and uncontrollable?

 A. Since Noah left, he has been without a proper influence
 B. Work camps are not a decent place to raise children
 C. Without a proper home, he will become rootless and lose his sense of the importance of family
 D. Manual labor is not good for such a young child

23. Why do the other children ostracize Ruthie when she first arrives at the government camp?

    A. She is from Oklahoma
    B. She bullies a girl on the croquet court
    C. She is caught stealing at the general store
    D. She is from a large family

24. At the cotton farm, where do the Joads live?

    A. In a boxcar
    B. In a shack
    C. In a tent
    D. In a culvert

25. At the end of the novel, Ma explains to Pa that some people live "in jerks," while others live in "all one flow." This is her way of describing an essential difference between which two groups?

    A. Rich and poor
    B. Oklahomans and Californians
    C. Men and women
    D. Tenant farmers and landowners

ANSWER KEY:

1: A; 2: C; 3: A; 4: C; 5: D; 6: C; 7: A; 8: A; 9: C; 10: A; 11: D; 12: B; 13: B; 14: D; 15: D; 16: B; 17: D; 18: B; 19: D; 20: D; 21: A; 22: C; 23: B; 24: A; 25: C

SUGGESTIONS FOR FURTHER READING

BLOOM, HAROLD, ed. *Modern Critical Interpretations of* THE
GRAPES OF WRATH. New York: Chelsea House Publishers, 1988.

FRENCH, WARREN, ed. *A Companion to* THE GRAPES OF WRATH.
New York: The Viking Press, 1963.

HAYASHI, TETSUMARO, ed. *Steinbeck's* THE GRAPES OF WRATH:
Essays in Criticism. Muncie, Indiana: Ball State University
Steinbeck Research Institute, 1990.

OWENS, LEWIS. THE GRAPES OF WRATH: *Trouble in the Promised
Land.* Boston: Twayne Publishers, 1989.

STEINBECK, JOHN. *Working Days: The Journals of* THE GRAPES OF
WRATH, 1938–1941. New York: The Viking Press, 1989.

WYATT, DAVID, ed. *New Essays on* THE GRAPES OF WRATH. New
York: Cambridge University Press, 1990.

REVIEW & RESOURCES